THE ARAB HORSE

GW00537750

CONTEN

INTRODUCTION

The Arabian is regarded as the oldest pure breed, but its exact origins remain unproven for lack of scientific evidence. A skeleton of a horse with a characteristically Arabian-type skull, discovered by archaeologists in the Sinai peninsular, has been dated to *c.* 1700 BC. This is the earliest physical evidence of a horse in Egypt.

Antique sculpture and ancient rock drawings depicting horses of Arabian appearance, found in the Arabian peninsular, as well as wall inscriptions in Egypt, confirm that an Arabian type has existed in the Middle East for well over 3,000 years. These Eastern, or Oriental, horses are considered to be the tap-root stock of all Southern hot-blooded equines, as opposed to the Northern cold-blooded.

HISTORY

Legends and traditions going back to 3,000 BC or earlier, and later recorded by numerous writers, support the belief that the first Arab horses came from Yemen. A Babylonian tablet, dating to *c.* 1,750 BC, provides the earliest written record. From Assyrian inscriptions we learn that King Sargon drove herds of horses from Arabia into Syria and that the Queen of Sheba presented King Solomon with an Arab mare named Safanad. King Solomon was one of the earliest known collectors of Arabians.

The Arabian was primarily a war-horse and early Arab writers and poets recounted the exploits and heroic deeds of Arab horsemen.

PRIDE OF OWNERSHIP

Admiration of the very best Arabians led those with power and wealth to acquire collections. Potentates through the Middle East successively assembled large studs, so that it be-came something of a status symbol to own the finest specimens.

Undoubtedly the most important influence on modern Arab horse breeding was that of Abbas Pasha I, Viceroy of Egypt 1848 – 54, from whose stock many present-day horses descend.

BEDOUIN BELIEFS AND BREEDERS

The Bedouin of Arabia believed that horses were indigenous to their country, whose peninsular was once watered and fertile; to them the Arabian is a breed apart, all others being considered *Kadish* (impure). It is feasible that herds did become isolated, and over centuries developed distinctive features, such as extremely dense bone.

Physical differences

The Arabian has certain unmistakable physical differences from other breeds and is notable for its perfect symmetry. The Bedouin most valued three characteristics: the exquisite head with large eyes and tapering muzzle; the graceful curve of the throat (*mitbah*); high tail carriage, indicating exceptional strength of back.

From earliest mention the Arabian was extolled for beauty and nobility but harsh desert conditions ensured that only the fittest survived to transmit genes tending to toughness and endurance.

Horse-breeding tribes

Ancestors of many of the famous horse-breeding tribes are said to have left Yemen

in AD 120. They moved northwards and then gradually spread over the whole of the northern part of the Arabian peninsular.

In tribal warfare and raids mares were used because stallions were more likely to neigh, alerting the enemy. Camels were ridden on the longer journeys, with mares led alongside and thus kept fresh for forays, where their courage, agility and endurance often saved their rider's life.

Close association with humans

Mares and foals lived in the camps, frequently sharing their owner's tent. From an early age foals were fed by hand, firstly on camel's milk alone, then grain would be introduced. Children played with the foals and the mares grew up with an affection for their human companions.

The Bedouin were always loath to part with their best mares, for they considered that the female line was the most important. For this reason the strain-name of every Arabian is that of its dam.

DISTRIBUTION AND DEVELOPMENT

During the sixteenth and seventeenth centuries many Eastern stallions and mares were brought into England and other European countries and mostly used to up-grade local stock.

Towards the end of the nineteenth century travellers had noted a scarcity of high-class horses in Arabia and those in England and other European countries, notably Poland and Germany, who were concerned about this, started pure-bred studs because they feared degeneration, or even extinction, within its land of origin.

INFLUENCE OF BRITISH-BRED ARABIANS

The United States and other countries became interested and many purchased

foundation stock from England, with the result that horses with British-bred ancestors can now be found in the stud books of practically every country where Arabians are bred.

Arab horses have been categorised as Egyptian, English, Polish, and so on – confusing definitions which merely mean that the individual is bred from stock raised in a specific country. Varying types did emerge, as can happen when breeders, pursuing individual ideals, emphasise respective characteristics.

POPULATION EXPLOSION

The emergence of the Arabian as a highly popular breed began after the Second World War. The most dramatic population explosion occurred in the United States. By 1950 registrations were approach-

ing a total of 5,000. During the 1970s American breeders imported large numbers of Arabians, notably from Egypt and Poland, and later from Russia, and by 1985 registrations had increased to over 400,000! Huge increases also occurred in most other countries – the boom years beginning in the 1960s.

CONFORMATION AND TYPE

The Arabian is the embodiment of equine quality. The fineness of its skin and coat is superior to all other breeds, and its elegance, dignity, style and intelligence make it a creature apart.

BREED STANDARD

The head
The head is one of the most important features, and is a hallmark of the breed, being

extremely refined and with great width across the forehead, wedge-shaped from the side, and broad across the cheekbones, tapering to a fine muzzle. The large dark eye is set low in the head; it is not a fault to show white around the eye. The jawbones are set wide apart, the mouth is quite long. A 'dish' in the profile below the eye is desirable but not essential. Extremely concave, or dished, heads were rare in desert-bred Arabians and were not considered important by the Arabs. Nostrils are large and delicately edged, capable of great expansion. The ears are finely chiselled and often with inward-curving tips; mares may have larger ears than stallions.

The neck

The neck is long and the throat beautifully modelled in a graceful curve. The head and neck are carried high and proudly; a mare's neck is lighter and often straighter than a stallion's, which usually has a pronounced crest.

The neck springs from the top of the chest, which is wide and deep, allowing ample heart room and a deep girth, ensuring stamina.

The shoulder

The shoulder is well laid back, long and clearly defined at the withers; good action is dependent on the slope and length of the shoulder blades, which allows the foreleg to swing freely backward and forward.

The back

The back is quite short and strong, though often longer in a mare. A slight concave line lies between the withers and the loins, which spring strongly in a curve to the quarters. The quarters should not be higher than the withers in adult horses, though growing youngsters may, temporarily, be higher behind than in front.

The ribs
The ribs are particularly round and well-sprung, the flank is set low, giving a close-coupled look.

The quarters
The quarters are long from the hip to the point of buttocks and wide across the hips and thighs. Gaskins and thighs are strongly muscled with great length from the stifles to the hocks, which are large and flat, with well-developed points and a straight drop of hind leg.

The tail
The tail is set on high and when the horse is in motion is carried in an arch or held like a flag, particularly when the animal is moving fast, or is excited. Slight sideways tail-carriage is acceptable.

The Arabian must stand over a lot of ground, with the forelegs set well forward, leaving the elbows clean and free. The forearm should be strongly muscled and long, with well set-down large flat knees and short cannon bones.

The hoofs are circular, dense, smooth and hard. Many good Arabians, like Thorough-breds, slightly turn out one or both hind feet when standing.

The coat
The coat is extremely fine and silky. Around the eyes and muzzle the hair is so sparse that skin-colour predominates. The skin is refined and black, pink under white markings. Manes and tails are long, fine and silky; thick bushy tails are not an Arab feature.

Colours
Colours are grey, chestnut, bay, brown and, rarer, black. Some chestnuts carry a lot of white hairs in their coat but roan is not an Arab colour. White markings, mostly on the head and legs, occasionally on the body, are often a notable feature.

Height
There is no height limit; 14.2 to 15.2 hh is usual, though many are larger or smaller. The average weight is from 850 to 1,000 lb (approximately 340 to 450 kg).

MOVEMENT
The movement is free and expressive, with good flexion of all the joints. Pride and spirit are the distinguishing characteristics,

evident when the horse is moving. The walk is fast and free, hind feet often over-stepping the front track by eight to twelve inches.

Trotting

The trotting action is exceptional, darting out from the shoulder with the hind legs swinging powerfully forward from the stifles and the hocks well lifted and going a trifle wide when seen from behind. The front feet should shoot out with a floating movement.

Cantering

The smooth and effortless canter is a speciality of the breed, together with an outstanding capacity for quick stopping and turning. The gallop is also free and light with a big stride.

INFLUENCE ON OTHER BREEDS

As an old pure breed the Arabian is extremely prepotent and for centuries has been used to up-grade other breeds, with the result that there is hardly a breed of light horse that does not contain some Arab blood.

THE THOROUGHBRED

The most famous and prolific breed to evolve from Arabian sources is the Thoroughbred. The foundation stock was an admixture of Eastern mares and stallions and Galloways and other British horses. Three phenomenal stallions – The Darley Arabian, the Godolphin Arabian and the Byerley Turk – dominated Thoroughbred ancestry and every Thoroughbred traces in the male line to just these three.

THE SHAGYA

The Shagya was selectively developed at the Babolna Stud in Hungary. It is of over 90 per cent Arab blood and is a popular breed in Europe and, more recently, the United States.

THE LIPIZZANER

The Lipizzaner, a well-known European breed containing much Arab blood, originated in the old stud at Lipica, in the former Yugoslavia, where the recording of horses from 1735 regulated the establishment of the breed.

PONY BREEDS

Pony breeds have also had intermittent infusions of Arab blood. In Britain this includes the New Forest, Dartmoor, and Welsh. The Welsh Mountain pony in particular shows much Arab quality, especially in its elegance and pretty head. The Scottish Highland and Irish Connemara also carry Arab blood.

The Austrian Haflinger, the Landais in France and the South African Basuto pony have all been influenced by the Arabian.

Show ponies

Many of today's British show ponies owe much to Arab blood. Pure-bred stallions and mares crossed with a variety of ponies have resulted in a large number of successful part-bred Arab show winners.

Part-bred horses also contribute to the success story of Arab crosses, for many have reached the top in various performance activities, including show jumping and eventing, as well as in hack and other show classes.

OTHER ARAB INFLUENCES

Numerous other herds around the world contain Arabian blood, including the Tersk in Russia and the 'wild' horses of the Camargue in France, the Gidran, and the Spanish Andalusian. The Hispano Arabe, a new breed, is the result of crossing Andalusian with Arabian.

American breeds influenced by Arabians include the Morgan and the Quarter Horse. The Australian Waler was evolved from Arabian, Barb, Dutch and Spanish ancestry.

TRAINING AND GENERAL MANAGEMENT

From its long association with man the Arab horse has inherited an ability to form strong attachments to humans; stallions can be extraordinarily gentle with children.

They are exceptionally intelligent and it should always be borne in mind that, although they learn very quickly, they also get bored easily if lessons lack variety.

FOAL TRAINING

Whilst still with its mother a foal can be given the basic lessons of compliance and good manners. It is a good idea to teach the foal to understand that when it is wearing a headcollar it must do as it is told but when this is removed it is free to play.

SLOW TO MATURE

Arabians are comparatively slow-maturing, and to allow them to develop fully and without physical harm they should not be backed until they are three years old. It is then advisable to leave them another year so regular work does not begin before they are four. To force them as youngsters and feed them up to become fat or heavy may well lead to problems later.

Plenty of fresh air and exercise are vital for Arab horses, not only when they are young but at any age. They do not take happily to a life mostly confined to a stable. This aspect is perhaps not fully understood and if problems ever arise, especially with stallions, more often than not it is due to the horse having insufficient freedom.

TRAINING FOR RIDDEN WORK

Serious work can begin at three years with lungeing and long-reining as a preparation for backing and the horse can be taught to listen to commands. Arabians do not forget their lessons; months can elapse and their education be resumed from exactly where it was left off.

It is a good idea to include schooling when out on a ride. Arabians are eager and willing to please and they have a great capacity for enjoying new ventures with their rider. Schooling in a set area can prove dull but, if included whilst out at exercise, lessons become much more interesting.

With their high intelligence Arabians are also more sensitive than most other breeds. Sometimes a horseman will find himself at odds with these qualities and unable to appreciate fully the individualistic nature; alternatively many people find that once they have ridden an Arabian they could never go back to another breed.

GENERAL CARE

Despite their fine skin and coat Arab horses are quite hardy and thrive on a 'natural' upbringing.

When they are at least two months old, foals can stay out at night in the warmer months but it is advisable to bring them in once a day for handling and a feed. If foals are used to a small amount of hard feed when with their mothers there should be no feeding problems at weaning.

Until maturity Arabians need to be stabled at night through the winter and well provided with hard feed plus hay but, provided they are on good grazing, do not need such extras during the summer, when they should be out all the time.

Open sheds in the paddocks are recommended. They are often most appreciated in the summer when flies are troublesome, and are useful shelters for mature horses during the winter, though stabling at night is advisable in severe weather. Hay should be fed during the winter months and hard feed provided for older mares. Brood mares and stallions need hard feed all the year round.

Arabians are good 'doers' and run to fat quite easily on rich early grass and, if they are not being exercised, care needs to be taken to prevent the risk of laminitis.

Regular worming, feet trimming and teeth care is, of course, essential routine for horses of every age. Here the needs of Arabians differ little from any horse, and sound advice on general care can be found in numerous good books on the subject.

PERFORMANCE

Arabians make perfect riding horses and although some may consider their lack of size a disadvantage they do not feel small to ride owing to their natural balance, good conformation and harmony of action.

ENDURANCE

It is generally acknowledged that the Arabian is the breed *par excellence* for endurance riding. Scientific tests have shown that its innate qualities of efficient heart, superior blood composition and endurance-orientated muscle fibre, surpass those of other breeds and prove it eminently suitable for this particular work. In addition its characteristic generosity and willingness to give the utmost make it the most popular choice. There are, of course, other breeds which have excelled in endurance but most can be found to carry Arabian blood in their veins. Arabians hold most of the records for total miles completed and many go on competing up to 'veteran' age. In most of the greatest rides, such as the Tevis Cup in the United States and the Quilty Cup in Australia, Arabians or their derivatives completely dominate the scene.

RACING

The Arabian is the swiftest pure breed because the Thoroughbred and the Quarter Horse (a breed which is fast over short distances) are both of mixed ancestry. Horse racing began in the Middle East.

Arabians have raced in Egypt, Syria and Persia for at least 1,000 years but it is only during the twentieth century that Arab horse racing has developed into a major sport.

Racing in the United Kingdom has been organised by the Arab Horse Society since 1978. From small beginnings enthusiasm grew rapidly and up to twenty meetings have been held every summer for pure-breds, Anglo-Arabs and part-breds.

In Britain, Arab racing under the AHS is essentially an amateur sport but run in a professional manner. Horses are not allowed to race until they are four years old. Arab racing now takes place in several European countries and many others around the world; in the United States it has become a major sport.

However, nowhere has the recent revival of flat racing been as dramatic as in the Gulf and the United Arab Emirates. From 1990 the number of meetings held and horses in training rose more rapidly than in any other part of the world and it has a large following.

MARATHONS

Marathon races, run over the Olympic distance of 26¼ miles, have been held by the Arab Horse Society since 1974. At this race-distance the Arabian can old its own against all comers and Anglo-Arabs also have a good success record. These races are becoming increasingly popular in the Gulf States where the Sheikhs enjoy a sport riding their own Arab horses.

DRESSAGE

Despite the fact that larger European breeds of horse still seem to be the most popular in the United Kingdom for dressage, a steadily increasing number of riders of Arabians are now competing in this discipline.

It is more common to see Arabians competing in open dressage competition against all breeds in countries outside Europe.

SHOW JUMPING

It is completely untrue to say, as some do, that Arab horses cannot jump, and there are many instances of pure-breds competing successfully in show jumping. In recent years the AHS has included show jumping at its National Show.

EVENTING

Across country and through water too they show great determination. It might be assumed that they are too small to tackle big courses but an Arabian of only 14.3 hh proved what can be achieved through consistent pluck by winning eventing championships in Norway and Finland.

However, the larger Anglo-Arabs and part-breds are more appreciated for eventing and several have competed at top level in recent years, including two which became members of British International teams. Their forte was jumping and they excelled in the cross-country section in particular.

A MOUNT FOR YOUNG PEOPLE

Arabians make very suitable mounts for young people, and in many countries are popular with Pony Club members, one reason being that they form strong bonds with their riders.

DRIVING

Arabians are driven singly
or in teams and in the
United States have
competed with success
in Combined Driving
Competitions.

SHOWING IN-HAND

All-Arabian shows are held
in every country where they
are bred, the highlight being
the country's National
Championships.

    Owing to the great num-
ber being bred, competition
has naturally intensified
and, with little to choose
between the top horses,
in-hand presentation has
inevitably become an
overemphasised angle of
showing. Whether this is
desirable for the good of
the breed is increasingly
debated. In many European
Arabian shows the ridden
horse has hardly been
considered at all.

THE VERSATILE ARABIAN

For their size, they have great weight-carrying
capacity and make ideal family horses, where
their undoubted versatility ensures their
participation in a wide variety of activities.
There is in fact very little that an Arab horse
cannot tackle. They were used for polo, pig-
sticking, hunting and gymkhanas, favourite
pastimes with Indian Army officers in the
nineteenth century, and they played an
additional role as chargers.

When 'presentation' means overfed
youngsters who have been confined so that
when out of their box they are excessively
'showy', or when there is use of drugs,
substances to raise tail carriage, and even
cosmetic interference with looks, the out-
look for the breed does not augur well.

    Another problem arising out of vastly
increased numbers and modern showing
fashions is the misconception that there are
two kinds of Arab horse: 'show' and 'performance'. Some think that winning in-hand

is what matters; conversely others regard race-track or endurance success as all important and may consider some 'show' horses unsuitable for ridden work, conformation having become secondary to extreme type. This dichotomy can confuse newcomers, for the ideal Arabian is both beautiful and practical, an all-rounder equal to show-ring and performance events.

SHOWING UNDER SADDLE

Classes for ridden Arabians are now held at many horse shows and the quality of the

entries has risen dramatically over the last decade, especially amongst the geldings and mares.

In the United Kingdom the judge is expected to ride all the entrants. Competition is extremely strong and a very high standard of schooling is expected.

WESTERN RIDING

Western riding is now gaining popularity in the United Kingdom, having been an important feature in American Arabian shows for many years.

Working hunter and other classes are often included at shows, and are open to Anglo-Arabs and part-breds as well. The population of Anglos is still comparatively small in the United Kingdom, whereas in France the breed is well known and one of the most popular choices.

ADVICE ON BUYING

CHOOSING AN ARABIAN FOR RIDING

Selecting an Arabian for performance has similarities with choosing a horse from another breed; special attributes should be well in evidence, together with good conformation and a clear indication of correct upbringing should all be carefully appraised.

Depending on the work for which you intend to use the horse, it is wise to study the close relatives and note their performance in the discipline of your choice.

Visit studs with a good record of producing performance horses. If buying a horse already broken in, ask about its past history as well as riding it. A veterinary examina-

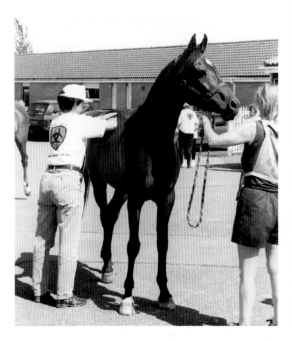

tion is always advisable; there can be 'hidden' defects only discoverable by a vet which might affect performance.

With any Arabian you consider purchasing, especially if you wish to breed or compete in AHS events, it is essential to make sure that the registration papers are in order so that transfers of ownership through the Society can be made.

SELECTING FOUNDATION STOCK

If your interest is in establishing a stud, careful and thorough preparation is required. Assuming that a preliminary review has been accomplished to provide background knowledge of the Arabian, books and magazines studied, and visits made to Arabian breed shows, it is then advisable to note individual horses you admire.

Do not assume that all you need do is go out and purchase several champion mares and sires and mate them to produce top winners – genetics do not work that way.

Start visiting the studs where the type of stock you like best is bred. A horse in show condition can look very different when seen loose in its home paddock, where it can best be judged in unconstrained action.

Disposition

Disposition is of course very important, and a walk round fields of brood mares and young stock will tell you far more about

their characters and the way they have been brought up than any visit to a yard of show horses, led out and stood up for your appraisal. You have to live with your horses all the year round, and if they impress in winter coats after a good roll on muddy ground you will know they will look even more beautiful when gleaming in the summer sunshine. Once your mind is made up regarding type and blood-lines, seek advice from a few knowledgeable breeders, and study the performance and show careers of specimens of the same blood-lines.

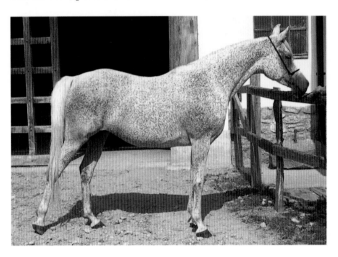

PROBLEMS

SCID (SEVERE COMBINED IMMUNODEFICIENCY)

SCID in Arabians came to light via clinical reports from Australia in the 1960s. Affected foals lack immune capacity and usually die from massive infections before the age of five months.

SCID test

Following extensive research, in 1997 a test was established which showed up SCID gene carriers. With the test available it is not necessary to remove from breeding all individuals possessing the gene, since only when two horses carrying it are mated can a SCID foal result, the chances being one in four. With scrupulous selection the gene's frequency will gradually decrease.

The SCID gene is not as prevalent as previously believed; at one time it was thought that 25 – 30 per cent of Arabians were affected. The latest results from the United States, where testing started, show that only 8.4 per cent possess the gene. It is strongly advised that all breeding stock, or at least all stallions, are blood-tested so that no two carriers are mated.

THE ARABIAN IN ART

The Arab horse with its pronounced beauty has long been the subject of various art forms. As early as 1600 BC, beautiful little horses of Arabian type are depicted on jewellery and other artifacts. Many rock inscriptions from around this period are also of this type.

The oral tradition in Arabia was highly honoured, and flourished several generations prior to Islam; many of the tales related were later put into verse by Arab poets.

Exquisitely illustrated Persian manuscripts show a stick-and-ball game – the forerunner of modern polo – with players mounted on horses with Arabian characteristics.

There are numerous paintings by artists over the last few centuries of Arabs with their steeds in oriental or desert settings. Pictures of this type are especially popular with Arab art collectors, and a number of modern artists follow the tradition.

PAINTINGS

The arrival of Eastern horses in Europe, and particularly of the Arabians who constituted the foundation stock of the Thoroughbred, resulted in many of them being painted by old masters.

SCULPTURE

The Arabian also appeals to sculptors, as countless bronzes testify, from small head studies to life-size or larger statues. Some members of the famous group of French artists know as 'Les Animaliers' chose the Arabian as their subject.

Amongst the statues of great historical figures one of the best known must surely be the Duke of Wellington seated on his famous part-bred charger Copenhagen, at Hyde Park Corner in London.

ACKNOWLEDGEMENTS

The author wishes to thank Diana Dykes for her assistance in the preparation of this book and all those who helped with photographs: Betty Finke, Eric Jones, Jane Kadri, The Mathaf Gallery Ltd., Pat Maxwell, Judith Ratcliff, Rik van Lent, Peter and Marilyn Sweet, Chris Whale and The Arab Horse Society.

British Library Cataloguing-in-Publication Data.
A catalogue record for this book is available from the British Library

ISBN 0.85131.800.2

Published in Great Britain in 2000 by
J. A. Allen an imprint of Robert Hale Ltd.,
Clerkenwell House, 45–47 Clerkenwell Green,
London EC1R 0HT

Design and Typesetting by Paul Saunders
Series editor Jane Lake
Colour processing by Tenon & Polert Colour Scanning Ltd., Hong Kong
Printed in Hong Kong by Dah Hua International Printing Press Co. Ltd.